Learn to Speak Zulu

George Poulos

12 INTRODUCTORY LESSONS

TARGET GROUP

CHILDREN AND ADULTS WHO HAVE
NO KNOWLEDGE OF THE ZULU LANGUAGE

Published by:
George Poulos
Centurion
South Africa
e-mail: gpoulog@yebo.co.za

web: www.linx.co.za/zulu

First Edition   1999

Second Edition 2003

Third Edition   2006

Fourth Edition   2018

Cover design by Lelanie Koumoutsaris

ISBN: 9781980337232

WHY YOU SHOULD LEARN ZULU

- Zulu is one of the official languages of South Africa.

- As a *mother-tongue,* Zulu is spoken by more people than any other language in South Africa. There are an estimated 11.6 million mother-tongue speakers of Zulu. Countless others speak it as a second language.

- Zulu belongs to the largest linguistic group of languages in South Africa, namely the Nguni group. One of the implications of this is that if you have a practical knowledge of Zulu, then you should be able to communicate to a certain extent with speakers of Ndebele, Xhosa and Swati. It is estimated that approximately 22 million people belong to the Nguni group.

TABLE OF CONTENTS

A note from the Author

Since the democratic elections of 1994, there has been a growing need to learn an African language within certain sectors of South African society. There is no doubt that this need will grow more and more as time moves on.

The linguistic and didactic approach that I have used in this book is one which gradually took shape in my lecturing career which began at the University of the Witwatersrand. That was where the foundations of my theoretical linguistic and phonetic knowledge were firmly laid. I was then able to apply this knowledge at Rhodes University as well as at the University of South Africa.

In an introductory book of this nature, I have tried to steer away from highly theoretical explanations as well as complex constructions, and have also avoided a detailed analysis of alternative forms, where they might occur. Complex constructions have been reserved for another publication, entitled *"A Linguistic Analysis of Zulu"*. The approach in this book has therefore been simplified for your purposes, allowing you to move at your own pace through the various lessons. I have also included a list of common expressions at the end of the work which you should consult as often as possible. Remember that practice makes perfect, so try and practise what you learn in the lessons, with Zulu speakers with whom you come into contact; and concentrate wherever possible on the pronunciation of forms. Good luck in this challenging endeavour!

On a personal note, I should like to express my indebtedness to my wife, Panayiota for her moral support while I was preparing this work for publication. My deepest appreciation also goes to my children Nicholas and Cleo whose love has been a constant source of inspiration for me.

George Poulos *BA Hons, MA (Witwatersrand), PhD (Rhodes)*

GREETINGS

and

THE STRUCTURE OF THE NOUN

This lesson is divided into two parts. In the first part we will concentrate on common greeting forms and then we will look at the structure of nouns in Zulu.

PART 1 - GREETINGS

HELLO!

The equivalent of the English "Hello!" which can be used at different times of the day and night is:

Sakubona!   when addressing one person

OR

Sawubona!

This form of greeting can be used at any time of the day and night. It therefore freely translates the English "hello" but also covers the greetings "good morning", "good afternoon" and "good evening".

- Note that a "k" written in Zulu is pronounced more like the English "g" in a word such as "go".

- The "a" is pronounced like the English "u" in "but".

- The Zulu "o" is pronounced with more rounding of the lips than the English "o", and is similar in sound to the "o" in "more".

Furthermore, you should try and remember one very common feature of the Zulu language when speaking it – the second last syllable of a word is usually pronounced with a certain amount of emphasis and length.

So in the above greeting, you should put a little more emphasis on the second last syllable /**bo**/, hence:

Sa – ku – bo –na !

Sa – wu – bo – na !

When you address more than one person, the **"ku"** or **"wu"** in the above forms is replaced by **"ni"**.

Sanibona!   When addressing more than one person

Alternatively this form may be used with the ending **"ni"**:

Sanibonani! (Pronounced in quick speech as something like:

"Sanbonaan!")

Remember to place more emphasis on the second last syllable:

Sa – ni- bo – na – ni!

HOW ARE YOU?

In order to express "how are you?" in Zulu, one can use the very simple expression:

Unjani?

Because this is a question, the voice tends to rise in pitch on the last syllable. Remember that the second last syllable is a little longer than the others, hence we have something like the following:

U – njaa – ni?

This expression is used when you are speaking to one person.

When addressing more than one person, the initial **"u"** is replaced by **"ni"**.

Ninjani?   **(ni –njaa – ni?)**

A very important observation that one can make about this type of question, is that in Zulu culture it is considered respectful to use a plural form even when speaking to one person. So for example, it would be preferable to use the form **"ninjani?"** and not **"unjani?"** when speaking to one person.

The thinking behind this is that a Zulu speaker when using the plural form is not only enquiring about the individual himself, but is actually showing respect and asking about his family also.

(The singular form would be quite in order when addressing a child for example).

Practise the following expressions:

Sakubona!/ Sawubona!   Hello!

Ninjani?   How are you?

To express "I am well" in Zulu, either a singular form:

Ngikhona

is used, or more preferably the following plural form where the speaker is in fact replying by saying "I" and my family are well:

Sikhona

So we can illustrate a possible discourse situation as follows, where Joji and Thandi are talking to one another.

Joji   :   **Sawubona Thandi!**

Thandi: **Sawubona Joji!**

Joji   :   **Ninjani?**

Thandi: **Sikhona. Nina ninjani?**

(Here Thandi has introduced a pronoun **"nina"** which expresses the idea of "you as for you", how are you?")

4

Joji   :   **Sikhona**

The pronouns for the second person singular and plural may also be used in greeting forms.

These are:

wena   in the singular,

and

nina   in the plural.

Thus instead of just saying **"unjani?"** you may use the pronoun **"wena"** as well:

Wena unjani?

Likewise, instead of just saying **"ninjani"** you may say:

Nina ninjani?

ALTERNATIVE FORMS

As with any greetings, alternative forms exist and these could be confusing to master at this stage. However, they will come naturally to you when you are exposed to them more and more.

If you feel that you would like to concentrate on the above forms first, then leave out this section until a later stage when you will feel more confident to use a variety of alternative forms.

For example, instead of the **"unjani?"** greeting, you can also ask:

Usaphila na?

and instead of **"ninjani?"** you can say:

Nisaphila na?

The corresponding answers to these would be:

Ngisaphila   instead of   **Ngikhona**

and

Sisaphila   instead of   **Sikhona**

(Note once again that the second last syllable is long. The Zulu **"ph"** is pronounced like the English "p" in "pen" and not like the English "ph" in "philosophy".

It is also common in Zulu to introduce the form **"yebo"** in answers to greeting forms. The word **"yebo"** literally means "yes", and is sometimes used as a "filler-in" or catch phrase in conversation. So, for example, instead of just saying **"ngisaphila"**, you could also say:

Yebo, ngisaphila

Remember that the pronouns for the second person may also be used in greeting forms. As mentioned before these are:

wena   in the singular, and

nina   in the plural

Thus one may also say:

Wena usaphila na?   in the singular, and

Nina nisaphila na?   in the plural

GOODBYE!

In order to express "goodbye" in Zulu, you will need to understand that various possible contexts may exist. In brief, two expressions are used in Zulu to express the idea of "goodbye", when speaking to one person, namely:

Sala kahle!

and

Hamba kahle!

Before discussing the actual use of these two terms in conversation, it would help to get a literal translation of each form:

Sala Kahle!   means   "stay well!"

Hamba kahle!   means   "go well!"

As the translation implies, **"Sala kahle"** is used to say goodbye to someone who is staying behind at the time of parting. Thus if you are leaving a room where you have been talking to someone and that person is staying behind in that room, then you will say **"Sala kahle"** to him. He or she in turn will say **"Hamba kahle"** to you because you are actually leaving the room.

Should you both be leaving the place where a conversation may have taken place then you would both say **"Hamba kahle!"** to each other. So, for example, if you have been speaking on a pavement and you both then part to go your different ways, each of you would say **"Hamba kahle"** to each other.

Should you be talking to more than one person, then you would use the following plural forms:

Salani kahle!

Hambani kahle!

A few notes on the pronunciation of the above forms:

Note once again that the **"k"** in **"kahle"** sounds more like the **"g"** in the English "go".

The **"hl"** in **"kahle"** is a strange sound to English speakers and should be treated merely as a combination of an **"h"** and an **"l"** sound. All too often, English speakers pronounce this combination as a kind of a **"shl"** sound and this is incorrect. (The voice counterpart of this sound is **"dl"**).

NOTES ON A FEW ADDITIONAL SOUNDS

Obviously, for you to speak the language well, you will need to master the sounds of the language. This only comes with practice and you should not feel disillusioned if, at first, you can't quite pronounce a sound correctly. You will in most cases still be understood, and your main concern while learning is to be understood by the other parties. Practice makes perfect and in this regard you should exercise as much patience as possible.

Zulu is one of the languages of South Africa which has the so-called click sounds.

These are written as follows:

c   x   q

The "c" click

The "c" click sound is one that you have probably produced while expressing disapproval. It involves a sucking action by placing the tip of the tongue against the back of the top teeth, and allowing the air to be sucked back suddenly.

Try and produce this sound between vowels, e.g.

aca,   ece,   ici,   oco,   ucu

The "x" click

With this click, the tip of the tongue is placed on the ridge above the top teeth, and the air is then suddenly sucked back through the side of the tongue.

Try and produce this click between vowels:

axa,   exe,   ixi,   oxo,   uxu

The "q" click

This is the most pronounced of all clicks. Place the tip of the tongue on the ridge above the top teeth and suck hard. Allow the tip of the tongue to move backwards and then quickly release the top of the tongue. A sucking action will result, like the popping of a cork.

Try and pronounce this click between vowels:

aqa,   eqe,   iqi,   oqo,   uqu

PART 2 - THE STRUCTURE OF THE NOUN

The structure of the noun in Zulu differs markedly from that in English. As a general rule, every noun in Zulu consists of a noun prefix and a noun stem. Look at the following example which translates the English "boy".

umfana   "boy"

This noun consists of two parts, namely a noun prefix **"um"** and a stem **"fana",** thus:

um + fana

(It should be mentioned that a prefix always occurs at the beginning of a word, as opposed to a suffix which occurs at the end.)

Note that there are no definite or indefinite artcles in Zulu. The noun above, namely **"umfana"** translates the English "the boy" or "a boy'. The exact meaning will be determined by the context in which the noun is used.

Plurals in Zulu are formed in a way that is very different from that which occurs in English. In English, as you know, a suffix is usually added to the noun, so the plural of an example such as "boy" is formed by merely adding an "s", thus "boys".

In Zulu, the prefix of the noun is replaced by another prefix in order to form a plural. Thus the plural of **"umfana"** is formed by replacing the **"um"** prefix by another prefix, **"aba"**. The plural of **"umfana"** is therefore:

abafana

Let's look at a few more nouns with the **"um"** prefix in the singular and then also consider their corresponding plural forms:

	Singular	Plural
child	**umntwana**	**abantwana**
woman	**umfazi**	**abafazi**

Unfortunately, not all singular nouns have an **"um"** prefix, and this is where the Zulu structure becomes slightly more complicated. There are many other prefixes that occur in the singular and such prefixes have their own corresponding plural forms.

Let's look at an example. The noun for a "servant" is **"isisebenzi"** which consists of the prefix **"isi"** and the stem **"sebenzi".**

isi + sebenzi

The plural form of this noun is *not* **"abasebenzi",** but rather **"izisebenzi"**, where the prefix **"izi"** is used.

izi + sebenzi

Because **"umfana"** and **"isisebenzi"** commence with different prefixes, we say that they belong to different classes. All nouns in Zulu belong to some or other class by virtue of their prefixes and there are quite a number of noun prefixes in Zulu. Obviously, with a lot of practice, you will automatically recognize the different classes by just looking at the beginning part, or the prefix of the noun.

Let's now consider the list of the possible prefixes that occur in Zulu, with the singular forms on the left and the corresponding plural forms on the right. (You must understand that in any language, exceptions always occur, but the general rules are the ones that you must concentrate on at the moment.)

To make things a little easier, numbers have been given to these prefixes, so we simply refer to them as prefixes of class 1, or 6 etc.

Note that there are some numbers that are left out. The reason for this is that this number system has been drawn up for the whole LANGUAGE FAMILY to which Zulu belongs. In some languages, such as Zulu, certain prefixes don't occur. So for example there is no number 12 or 13 in the list below, but these two classes do occur in some of the other languages spoken north of our borders.

Another observation that might worry you is that class 1 and class 3 appear to have the same prefix. This is true but they are put into different classes for the following reasons:

- The nouns in class 1 are personal; they refer to some or other person and have a plural in class 2.

    EXAMPLE: **umfana** "boy"   **abafana** "boys"

    umntwana "child"   **abantwana** "children"

- The nouns in class 3 are impersonal; they have their plurals in class 4.
-

    EXAMPLE: **umfula** "river"   **imifula** "rivers"

    umkhonto "spear"   **imikhonto** "spears"

(Also note that classes 1a and 2a are treated as separate classes to those of 1 and 2 respectively. There are *theoretical* reasons why these are treated as 1a and 2a, and we need not delve into such details here).

NOUN CLASSES

SINGULAR		PLURAL	
1	um	2	aba
1a	u	2a	o
3	um	4	imi
5	i	6	ama
7	isi	8	izi
9	in/im	10	izin/izim
11	u		Takes plural in class 10
14	ubu		No plural
15	uku		No plural

Let's now consider examples of nouns in each of the above classes:

Class 1 with plural in class 2

umfana	"boy"	**abafana**	"boys"
umfazi	"woman"	**abafazi**	"women"
umlimi	"farmer"	**abalimi**	"farmers"
umntwana	"child"	**abantwana**	"children"

Class 1a with plural in class 2a

ubaba	"my father"	**obaba**	"our fathers"
umama	"my mother"	**omama**	"our mothers"
uthisha	"teacher"	**othisha**	"teachers"
unesi	"nurse"	**onesi**	"nurses"

Class 3 with plural in class 4

umsebenzi	"work"	**imisebenzi**	"types of work"
umfula	"river"	**imifula**	"rivers"
umlomo	"mouth"	**imilomo**	"mouths"
umkhonto	"spear"	**imikhonto**	"spears"

Class 5 with plural in class 6

ikhaya	"home"	**amakhaya**	"homes"
ithuba	"opportunity"	**amathuba**	"opportunities"
itafula	"table"	**amatafula**	"tables"
iphoyisa	"policeman "	**amaphoyisa**	"police"
ivila	"lazy person"	**amavila**	"lazy people"

Some neutral nouns occur in class 6 and they do not have a corresponding singular form, e.g.:

amandla	"strength, power"
amanzi	"water"
amafutha	"fat"

Class 7 with plural in class 8

isikole	"school"	**izikole**	"schools"
isikhathi	"time"	**izikhathi**	"times"
isisebenzi	"servant"	**izisebenzi**	"servants"

Class 9 with plural in class 10

indlu	"hut"	**izindlu**	"huts"
imoto	"motor car"	**izimoto**	"motor cars"
ingadi	"garden"	**izingadi**	"gardens"
intombi	"maiden, girl of marriageable age"	**izintombi**	"maidens, girls"
indaba	"matter"	**izindaba**	"matters"
insizwa	"young man"	**izinsizwa**	"young men"

A few nouns in this class take a plural in class 6 with prefix **ama**, e.g.:

indoda	"man"	**amadoda**	"men"
inkosi	"chief"	**amakhosi**	"chiefs"

(The **"h"** after the **"k"** in the last example merely indicates that the **"k"** is pronounced with quite a lot of air passing through the mouth after the **"k"** is released, very much like the English "k". A **"k"** after a nasal as in **inkosi** is also pronounced like the English "k").

Class 11 with plural in class 10

ukhuni	"firewood"	**izinkuni**	"pieces of firewood"
ukhezo	"spoon"	**izinkezo**	"spoons"
ufudu	"tortoise"	**izimfudu**	"tortoises"

Class 14

ubuntu   "human nature, values reflective of a culture"

ubudoda   "manhood"

ubusuku   "night"

ubuhlungu   "pain"

Class 15   (Nouns ae rarely found in this class)

ukudla   "food"

Adoptive nouns

As you may have noted in some of the above examples, numerous words in Zulu have been adopted from other languages, most notably, English and Afrikaans. This is as a result of contact with speakers of these two languages. Thus it is not at all surprising that many items and concepts that are characteristic of Western civilization have found their way into a language such as Zulu. When a noun is adopted into Zulu it undergoes some changes in order to fit into the word and sound structure of Zulu. So for example, an initial sound in an English word, could become part of a Zulu noun prefix, since all nouns in Zulu contain noun prefixes. Note for example how the English word "stool" is adopted into Zulu, to become:

isitulo

The initial sound in the English word is "s", and a Zulu speaker knows that the only noun prefix that contains this sound is that of class 7, namely **"isi"**. Thus the English "s" takes on a vowel "i" before and after it, when adopted into Zulu, thus **"isi"**. The rest of the English word "tool" is then also adapted to fit in with the sound structure as well as the word structure of Zulu. We know from research that nouns in Zulu end in a vowel and thus a vowel would have to come at the end, and in this case it is **"o"**.

The closest Zulu sound to the vowel in "tool" is the Zulu **"u"**. Thus the final result is:

isi + tulo > isitulo

Here are a few more examples of adoptive nouns in Zulu. Note that each noun contains a prefix, and therefore belongs to a class.

itafula	"table" (from Afr."tafel")	5
imoto	"motor car"	9
isikole	"school"	7
utamatisi	"tomato"	1a
uletisi	"lettuce"	1a
ubhanana	"banana"	1a
ibhasi	"bus"	5
ibhuku	"book"	5
i-ofisi	"office"	5
ijele	"jail"	5
isitofu	"stove	7
usawoti	"salt"	1a
umshini	"machine"	3
isipunu	"spoon"	7
ifulethi	"flat"	5
imayini	"mine"	9

THE STRUCTURE OF SENTENCES
(the present tense)

In the previous lesson, you were introduced to the noun and it was clearly shown how the structure of nouns in Zulu differs from that which occurs in English.

In this lesson, we will see how nouns can combine with verbs to form simple sentences.

One very significant observation that was made in the previous lesson concerning nouns, is the fact that there are many classes in Zulu. This is an important fact that you must remember when you try and form sentences in Zulu.

By way of introduction, let us look at a very simple sentence in English.

The boy studies Zulu

In this sentence, we have a noun "boy" which is the subject followed by the verb "studies", and finally we also have an object noun, namely "Zulu".

Now let's look at the Zulu counterpart of the above sentence:

Umfana ufunda isiZulu

Here the subject noun is **"umfana",** the verb is **"ufunda":** and the object noun is **"isiZulu".**

The structure of the verb in Zulu is rather complicated. This is because there are so many prefixes and suffixes which can be brought together to form a verb.

In the above Zulu example, **"ufunda"** can in fact be broken down as follows:

u + funda

"funda" is the actual part that conveys the idea of "study", and is sometimes called a verb stem.

In fact, if the structure of the Zulu verb was similar to that of English, then we would have something like the following:

*Umfana   funda

But there is a **"u"** that appears in the Zulu verb, and we have to explain this.

This **"u"** is what is generally called an "agreement marker"; and that is exactly what it does:

IT MARKS AGREEMENT

In this case it "marks agreement" with the subject of the verb, **"umfana"**.

As was clearly stated in the previous lesson, there are a number of noun classes in Zulu. **"Umfana"** for example is a noun that belongs to class 1.

In Zulu, the verb ***must show agreement*** with the noun class and it does so by means of an agreement marker. In fact this implies that there is an agreement marker for every class. So for example, we can say that **"u"** is the subject agreement marker for class 1. Whenever we have a noun in subject position which belongs to class 1 then the verb will always commence with **"u"**.

Look at the following examples:

Umfana	**ufunda**	**isiZulu**	-	The boy studies Zulu
Umfazi	**ufunda**	**isiZulu**	-	The woman studies Zulu

As the class of the subject noun changes, so does the form of the agreement marker.

For example, if we were to put the above subject nouns into the plural, then the form of the agreement marker would change. The plurals of the above nouns are **"abafana"** and **"abafazi"** respectively, and we know that these two nouns belong to class 2.

Thus an agreement marker for class 2 would have to be used, and in Zulu, the agreement marker for class 2 is **"ba"**.

| Abafana | **ba**funda | isiZulu | - | The boys study Zulu |
| Abafazi | **ba**funda | isiZulu | - | The women study Zulu |

Now let's look at the agreement markers in the other classes:

AGREEMENT MARKERS

SINGULAR	PLURAL
1 u	2 ba
1a u	2a ba
3 u	4 i
5 li	6 a
7 si	8 zi
9 i	10 zi
11 lu	Plural same as 10
14* bu	No plural
15 ku	No plural

(*Remember that there are no classes 12 and 13 in Zulu.)

Now let's look at a few examples where the subject noun occurs in different classes:

Obviously, if we use the verb stem **"-funda"** which means study, then only personal nouns can be used as subjects. Personal nouns only occur in certain classes.

Note one very interesting observation in the examples below, which is so typical of the Zulu language. The agreement marker normally contains at least one sound that is identical to that of the corresponding noun prefix. This is sometimes referred to as alliteration. (An exception is class 2a).

umfana	**u**funda	**isiZulu**	-	the boy studies Zulu
abafana	**ba**funda	**isiZulu**	-	the boys study Zulu
umama	**u**funda	**isiZulu**	-	my mother studies Zulu
omama	**ba**funda	**isiZulu**	-	our mothers study Zulu
iphoyisa	**li**funda	**isiZulu**	-	the policeman studies Zulu
amaphoyisa	**a**funda	**isiZulu**	-	the policemen study Zulu
isisebenzi	**si**funda	**isiZulu**	-	the servant studies Zulu
izisebenzi	**zi**funda	**isiZulu**	-	the servants study Zulu
insizwa	**i**funda	**isiZulu**	-	the young man studies Zulu
izinsizwa	**zi**funda	**isiZulu**	-	the young men study Zulu

Let's now look at a consolidated list of noun prefixes and agreement markers, and note the similarities that exist between these two lists.

At this stage, concentrate mainly on the classes that have personal nouns, i.e. classes 1, 2, 5, 6, 7, 8, 9 and 10.

Note that the agreement markers for 1a and 2a are the same as those for 1 and 2 respectively.

NOUN PREFIX		AGREEMENT MARKER
1	um	u
2	aba	ba
1a	u	u
2a	o	ba
3	um	u
4	imi	i
5	i	li
6	ama	a
7	isi	si
8	izi	zi
9	in/im	i
10	izin/izim	zi
11	u	lu
14	ubu	bu
15	uku	ku

PERSONS

There are six more agreement markers that can occur in sentences. These are the agreement markers which refer to the persons. In other words they are used when the subject is one of the following:

I, we, you (singular and plural), he, they

24

The Zulu agreement markers for these are:

I	**ngi**
We	**si**
You (singular)	**u**
You (plural)	**ni**
He/she	**u**
They	**ba**

Note now how we construct sentences with these agreement markers.

<u>ngi</u>funda	isiZulu	-	I study Zulu
<u>si</u>funda	isiZulu	-	we study Zulu
<u>u</u>funda	isiZulu	-	you (singular) study Zulu
<u>ni</u>funda	isiZulu	-	you (plural) study Zulu
<u>u</u>funda	isiZulu	-	he/she studies Zulu
<u>ba</u>funda	isiZulu	-	they study Zulu

You may note that the Zulu form of the second person singular and that of the third person singular are identical. This is so, except for a slight change in the tone. Perhaps it can just be mentioned that with the third person singular form, the pitch of the voice is raised.

MORE ON THE STRUCTURE OF SENTENCES

Up to now, we have looked at a rather simple sentence structure, for example:

umfana ufunda isiZulu - the boy studies Zulu

This sentence is in the present tense and consists of:

a subject noun   -   **umfana**

a verb   -   **ufunda**

an object noun   -   **isiZulu**

There is even a simpler structure than this, namely one that does not have an object noun, for example:

The boy studies

In Zulu one would expect the following:

*Umfana ufunda

However, this is not quite right, because there is a general rule in Zulu which states that if the verb is in the present tense, and *if it is not followed by an object noun,* then you must add **"ya"** after the agreement marker. (This is sometimes referred to as the long form).

Umfana uyafunda   -   the boy studies

Incidentally, the English present tense can also be expressed by:

The boy is studying

...where the verb "to be" is used, followed by the verb ending in "ing. This observation would apply to all the translations so far.

Now let's look at a few more examples where there is no object noun.

abafana bayafunda	-	the boys are studying
umama uyafunda	-	my mother is studying
iphoyisa liyafunda	-	the policeman is studying
isisebenzi siyafunda	-	the servant is studying
insizwa iyafunda	-	the young man is studying

And what about the persons?

The same applies:

ngiyafunda	-	I am studying
uyafunda	-	he is studying
bayafunda	-	they are studying

NOUNS AND VERB STEMS THAT YOU CAN START LEARNING

Nouns

Names of people go into class 1a. (English names usually remain unchanged and the prefix **"u"** is just added; some, however, undergo a slight change to fit in with the Zulu sound system.)

uSipho

uThemba

uThandi

uStephen

uJoji (from George)

umngane	"friend"	1
umuntu	"person"	1
umfowethu	"my brother"	1
udokotela	"doctor"	1a
umese	"knife"	3
ibhasi	"bus"	5
ivila	"lazy person"	5
isitolo	"store, shop"	7
isinkwa	"bread"	7
inyama	"meat"	9
inja	"dog"	9
intombazana	"girl"	9
ubisi	"milk"	11
ubuso	"face"	14
ukudla	"food"	15

Verb stems

funa	"want"
khuluma	"talk"
sebenza	"work"
phuza	"drink"
shaya	"hit"
gula	"be sick"
bona	"see"
thanda	"like, love"

hamba	"leave"'
khala	"cry, complain"
funda	"study, read"
pheka	"cook"
phuma	"come from"
thenga	"buy"
siza	"help"

Now translate the following sentences into Zulu using all the information given to you in this lesson:

1. Sipho is studying.

2. The doctor is leaving.

3. My brother is ill.

4. The girl is cooking.

5. My mother is studying Zulu.

6. Thandi is buying milk.

7. The lazy person is sick.

8. The boys are crying.

9. I am cooking meat.

10. You are working.

Answers

1. USipho uyafunda.

2. Udokotela uyahamba.

3. Umfowethu uyagula.

4. Intombazana iyapheka.

5. Umama ufunda isiZulu.

6. UThandi uthenga ubisi.

7. Ivila liyagula.

8. Abafana bayakhala.

9. Ngipheka inyama.

10. Uyasebenza.

LESSON 3

ASKING QUESTIONS

In Lesson 2, we looked at the way in which present statements can be expressed in Zulu. Of course, as is the case in any language, questions can also be asked, and these are discussed here. At this stage, we shall only be looking at questions which are in the present form.

The most common type of question in Zulu is one where the word **na?** is added at the end of the sentence, with a slight raising of the pitch on this **na.** Thus, for example, we know that the following statement:

Umfana uyafunda

Translates the English:

The boy is studying.

In order to ask the question:

Is the boy studying?

.....all we do is add **na?** after the verb, thus:

Umfana uyafunda na?

Note that the long form of the verb is used if **na?** immediately follows the verb.

If we take our earlier examples, in the previous lesson, we can change them all into questions by just adding **na?**

Statements

1. USipho uyafunda

2. Udokotela uyahamba

3. Umfowethu uyagula

4. Intombazana iyapheka

5. Umama ufunda isiZulu

6. UThandi uthenga ubisi

7. Ivila liyagula

8. Abafana bayakhala

9. Ngipheka inyama

10. Uyasebenza

Questions

1. **USipho uyafunda na?**

   Is Sipho studying?

2. **Udokotela uyahamba na?**

   Is the doctor leaving?

3. **Umfowethu uyagula na?**

   Is my brother ill?

4. **Intombazana iyapheka na?**

   Is the girl cooking?

5. **Umama ufunda isiZulu na?**

   Is my mother studying Zulu?

6. **UThandi uthenga ubisi na?**

   Is Thandi buying milk?

7. **Ivila liyagula na?**

   Is the lazy person ill?

8. **Abafana bayakhala na?**

   Are the boys crying?

9. **Ngipheka inyama na?**

   Am I cooking meat?

10. **Uyasebenza na?**

    Are you working?

Asking the question "when?"

When one wants to ask this question, the Zulu **"nini"** is used. Unlike in English, **"nini?"** occurs after the verb.   If there is an object, then **"nini?"** occurs at the end of the sentence (as a general rule).

Umfana ufunda isiZulu

The boy studies Zulu

becomes:

Umfana ufunda isiZulu nini?

When does the boy study Zulu?

Uyasebenza

He is working

Usebenza nini?

When does he work?

Note that with **nini?**, the short form of the verb (i.e. the form without **ya**) is used. Note also the following examples:

Uvuka nini?

When do you wake up?

Badla nini?

When do they eat?

Basebenza nini?

When do they work?

Isitshudeni sifunda nini?

When does the student study?

Niphuza itiye nini?

When do you (plural) drink tea?

UThandi udla nini?

When does Thandi eat?

Asking the question "what?"

When asking this question, **ni?** is added immediately after the verb. This **ni?** is more like a suffix and is added to the verb. Here the short form of the verb is used.

Ufunani?

What do you want?

Uphuzani?

What are you drinking?

Umfana ufundani?

What is the boy studying?

Asking the question "where?"

When asking this question, **phi?** is added immediately after the verb.

Uyaphi?

Where are you going?

Basebenzaphi?

Where do they work?

Uhlalaphi?

Where do you live?

Asking the question who/whom?

The Zulu question word for "whom?" is **ubani?**

Uthanda ubani?

Who(m) do you like?

Note that who(m)? in this sentence actually functions as the object of the verb, and in Zulu it comes after the verb. (Literally: You like whom?)

Nifuna ubani?

Who(m) do you (pl.) want?

Babona ubani?

Who(m) do they see?

When who? functions as the subject of the verb, then a more complicated construction is used. (A few such examples will be given later under 'Some Common Expressions').

LESSON 4

EXPRESSING REQUESTS AND COMMANDS

There are various ways in which requests and commands can be expressed in Zulu. We will deal with these separately here.

REQUESTS

When asking for something from one person, you may use the prefixes **"ma + wu"** before the verb stem which in this construction ends in **"e"**. For example, if you take the verb stem:

-ngena   *which means*   "enter, come in"

Then you would prefix **"ma + wu"** to it, and replace the final **"a"** with **"e"**.

Mawungene!

Which would convey the request:

"Please enter!"   *or*   "Please come in!"

Let's take another example:

Phuza   *meaning*   "drink"

This would become:

Mawuphuze amanzi!   "Please drink water!"

(It should be noted that there are also other ways of expressing requests, but these could be confusing to you at the introductory level")

Study the following verb stems again and then try the examples which follow:

siza	*meaning*	"help"
thenga	*meaning*	"buy"
hamba	*meaning*	"leave"
pheka	*meaning*	"cook"

Remember also the following nouns:
intombazana "girl", **isinkwa** "bread", **ukudla** "food".

Examples

Please buy bread!

Please leave!

Please help the girl!

Please cook the food!

Answers

Mawuthenge isinkwa!

Mawuhambe!

Mawusize intombazana!

Mawupheke ukudla!

The negative way of expressing a polite request is a little more complicated, and consists of the following:

The prefix **ma + wu** plus the prefix **nga**

...followed by the verb stem which here ends in **"i"**

So if we take the basic stem **"ngena"**, our negative construction would look like this:

Ma + wu + nga + ngeni

Mawungangeni!   Please do not come in!

Now try the negative equivalents of each of the positive forms given earlier:

Please do not buy bread!

Please do not leave!

Please do not help the girl!

Please do not cook the food!

Answers

Mawungathengi isinkwa!

Mawungahambi!

Mawungasizi intombazana!

Mawungapheki ukudla!

In each of the above examples, the request is directed to one person. Should you wish to address more than one person then you need to replace the **"wu"** in the prefix with **"ni"**, for example:

Please come in!   to more than one person

Maningene!   (Ma + <u>ni</u> + ngene)

The same would apply to the negative:

Maningangeni!   (Ma + ni + nga + ngeni)

A *command* is always considered to be more abrupt than a request. It is used only in certain contexts, for example, when one is addressing children. The construction is very simple and consists of the verb stem only, obviously with the correct pitch of voice that is usually associated with commands. Consider the following examples:

Ngena!   Enter, Come in!

Khuluma!   Speak!

Phuza!   Drink!

Pheka!   Cook!

Note an irregular form occurs with the verb stem **"za"**, which means "come". In order to command one to "come", the form that is used is:

Woza!

When addressing more than one person, the suffix **"ni"** is merely added to the above:

Ngenani!

Khulumani!

Phuzani!

Phekani!

Wozani!

Negative commands are more complicated and are made up as follows:

Musa   uku   +   verb stem!

Examples

Musa ukungena!	Don't come in!
Musa ukuphuza!	Don't drink!
Musa ukukhuluma!	Don't speak!

When addressing more than one person **"musa"** becomes **"musani"**.

Musani ukungena!	Don't come in!
Musani ukuphuza!	Don't drink!
Musani ukukhuluma!	Don't speak!

THE FUTURE AND PAST TENSES

In Lesson 2, we looked at the way in which sentences are structured in Zulu and we looked at examples in the present tense only. As you know, actions can take place in the future as well, or they may have taken place in the past. In this chapter, we shall look at the way in which Zulu expresses these two tenses.

THE FUTURE TENSE

This tense expresses an action which will take place at some time in the future. It is formed in the following way:

The Agreement Marker occurs first, followed by **"zo"** and then comes the verb stem. It is the **"zo"** which expresses future time in Zulu. To summarise, we may set this out as follows: (**AM** = Agreement Marker)

AM - zo - verb stem

So if you wish to express the following:

I will study

you would first use the AM for the first person **"ngi"** followed by **"zo"**, and then the verb stem **"funda"**, hence:

Ngizofunda

Let's now look at a few more examples:

As part of revision, the corresponding present tense form is given first and then the future tense:

IN EVERY CASE, REMEMBER THE RULES OF AGREEMENT. THE **AM** ALWAYS AGREES IN CLASS WITH THE SUBJECT NOUN.

PRESENT TENSE	FUTURE TENSE
Umfana ufunda isiZulu The boy studies Zulu	**Umfana uzofunda isiZulu** The boy will study Zulu
Udokotela uyahamba The doctor is leaving	**Udokotela uzohamba** The doctor will leave
Intombazana ipheka ukudla The girl is cooking food	**Intombazana izopheka ukudla** The girl will cook food
UThandi uthenga ubisi Thandi is buying milk	**UThandi uzothenga ubisi** Thandi will buy milk
Abafana bayakhala The boys are crying	**Abafana bazokhala** The boys will cry

PRESENT TENSE	FUTURE TENSE
Ngipheka inyama I am cooking meat **Umfana ushaya inja** The boy is hitting the dog	**Ngizopheka inyama** I will cook meat **Umfana uzoshaya inja** The boy will hit the dog

THE PAST TENSE

The past tense, as the name implies indicates an action that took place in the past. Its structure is as follows:

AM - VERB STEM where the **"a"** suffix is replaced by **"ile"**.

Thus if we wanted to say:

He has left

...then we would first use the AM **"u"** followed by the verb stem for "leave".

"hamba" which now becomes **"hambile"**.

Remember: **hamba   >   hambile**

So we have:

Uhambile

Now let's use the following verb stems in the past tense:

-khala   "cry"

-funda   "study, read"

-gijima   "run"

-dla   "eat"

-fika   "arrive"

As part of revision, the corresponding present tense form is given first and then the past tense:

PRESENT TENSE	PAST TENSE
Umfana uyakhala The boy is crying	**Umfana ukhalile** The boy cried
Intombazana iyafunda The girl is studying	**Intombazana ifundile** The girl has studied
Siyagijima We are running	**Sigijimile** We have run
Umfowethu uyadla My brother is eating	**Umfowethu udlile** My brother has eaten
Uthisha uyafika The teacher is arriving	**Uthisha ufikile** The teacher has arrived

You might remember that with the present tense, a shortened version of the verb was used when the verb was followed by an object. Well, the same situation exists in the past tense.

Generally speaking, the shortened version has a suffix **"-e"** rather than **"-ile"**.

Compare the following examples:

LONG FORM	SHORT FORM
Umfana udlile The boy has eaten **Intombazana ifundile** The girl has studied	**Umfana udle inyama** The boy has eaten meat **Intombazana ifunde isiZulu** The girl has studied Zulu

It should be noted that the short form of the verb is also used before certain adverbs, especially manner adverbs. Time adverbs on the other hand, may be preceded by either the short or the long form; the long form is usually associated with a certain amount of emphasis:

Manner adverb: **kakhulu** "much, a lot"

Abafana bakhalile   **Abafana bakhale kakhulu**

The boys cried   The boys cried a lot

Time Adverb: **izolo** "yesterday"

Abafana bakhal<u>ile</u>

The boys cried

Abafana bakhal<u>e</u> izolo

The boys cried yesterday

or

Abafana bakhal<u>ile</u> izolo

The boys did cry yesterday

TO EXPRESS CERTAIN 'PRESENT' STATES

One of the more difficult verb forms to learn in Zulu concerns the expression of certain states.

In Zulu, a present state such as:

I am hungry

.....is not expressed by the present tense, but rather by a verb that looks very much like the past tense above. There are very interesting reasons why this is the case, but this would be too theoretical to explain here. Only some verbs occur in this way. With most verbs, the ordinary present tense is used as was seen earlier.

It is perhaps best for you to learn by heart some of the most common verbs that are affected in this way. These are as follows. Note that in some cases, the **"ile"** suffix is used. In other cases, irregular forms ending in **"e"** occur.

STATE FORM		VERB STEM
-lambile	"be hungry"	-lamba
-omile	"be thirsty"	-oma
-khathele	"be tired"	-khathala
-thukuthele	"be angry"	-thukuthela
-dakiwe	"be drunk"	-dakwa
-lele	"be asleep"	-lala

Now look at the following sentences:

Ngilambile   "I am hungry"

Abafana bomile   "The boys are thirsty"

(Note here that the Agreement Marker, **"ba"** has become **"b"** before a vowel **"o"**.)

Umfana ukhathele   "The boy is tired"

Uthisha uthukuthele   "The teacher is angry"

Isitshudeni sidakiwe   "The student is drunk"

UThandi ulele   "Thandi is sleeping"

(As a conclusion to this section, it may be mentioned that there are also other ways of expressing past actions in Zulu. However, an explanation of these would be confusing to you at the "introductory level".)

THE USE OF ADVERBS

As is the case in English, Zulu has different types of Adverbs, the most frequent ones being Adverbs of Time, Place and Manner.

Consider the following:

Adverbs of Time

manje	"now"
izolo	"yesterday"
namhlanje	"today"
kusasa	"tomorrow"

The use of adverbs in sentences is rather straightforward, and as a general rule they follow the English word order:

Please leave now!

Manihambe manje!

I will leave tomorrow

Ngizohamba kusasa

Mother saw the teacher yesterday

Umama ubone uthisha izolo

I will help Themba today

Ngizosiza uThemba namhlanje

Adverbs of place

Adverbs of place are formed in various ways. There are a few basic rules in deriving such forms, and these are mentioned here as well. Some adverbs of place should be learnt by heart, since the rules can be confusing in certain cases. A few examples are given below. Note that the English translations may include the prepositions "at", "to" "from", etc. Note also that prepositions do not occur as separate words in Zulu. The choice of English preposition will depend on the context and the verb that is used.

With nouns commencing in **"i"** or **"u"**, the adverb prefix **"e"** replaces the **"i"** or **"u"**; and sometimes a suffix **"eni"** or **"ini"** is used. In the examples below, **"eni"** is used with a noun ending in **"a"** and **"e'** and **"ini"** with a noun ending in **"i"**. There are some words that do not take a suffix at all. You will need to learn these by heart.

ADVERBS		NOUNS	
edolobheni	"at, to, from town"	<	**idolobha**
esikoleni	"at, to, from school"	<	**isikole**
emfuleni	"at, to, from the river"	<	**umfula**
emsebenzini	"at, to, from work"	<	**umsebenzi**
esitolo	"at, to, from the store/shop"	<	**isitolo**
ekhaya	"home"	<	**ikhaya**
eyunivesithi	"at, to, from university"	<	**iyunivesithi**

With personal and proper nouns, the prefix **"ku"** is merely added:

ADVERBS		NOUNS
kuJoli	"to, from George"	< uJoji
kuThemba	"to, from Themba"	< uThemba
kumfana	"to, from the boy"	< umfana
kumama	"to, from mother"	< umama
kunesi	"to, from the nurse"	< unesi

Consider also the following place names:

ADVERBS		NOUNS
ePitoli	"at, to, from Pretoria"	< iPitoli
eGoli	"at, to, from Johannesburg"	< iGoli
eThekwini	"at, to, from Durban"	< iTheku

Note the use of the prefix **"kwa"** instead of **"e"**, in the following place name:

KwaZulu   at, to, from Zululand   <   **uZulu**

Consider a few sentence examples now:

The boys are going to school (i.e. they are on their way)

Abafana baya esikoleni

They work in Johannesburg

Basebenza eGoli

The students are studying at the university

Izitshudeni zifunda eyunivesithi

He is going to the nurse

Uya kunesi

<u>Adverbs of Manner</u>

kakhulu   "a lot, much"

kabi   "badly"

kahle   "well"

Look at the following sentences:

Themba studies a lot

UThemba ufunda kakhulu

Thandi works badly

UThandi usebenza kabi

The teacher speaks well

Uthisha ukhuluma kahle

How to express the notion of "with, together with"

Here we are looking at sentences such as:

Thandi works with Themba

Granny is walking with the dog

I study together with the boys

The prefix in such cases is **"na"**. This would in effect mean that **"na"** occurs before nouns such as **"uThemba", "inja" and "abafana"** in the above sentences. However, in Zulu, two vowels cannot occur next to one another. Instead there is a merging of vowels, as follows:

na	**+**	**u**	**>**	**no**
na	**+**	**i**	**>**	**ne**
na	**+**	**a**	**>**	**na**

Thus:

na	**+**	**uThemba**	**>**	**noThemba**
na	**+**	**inja**	**>**	**nenja**
na	**+**	**abafana**	**>**	**nabafana**

The above sentences would thus be translated as follows:

Thandi works with Themba

UThandi usebenza noThemba

Granny is walking with the dog

Ugogo uhamba nenja

I study together with the boys

Ngifunda nabafana

How to express "by means of"

Here we are looking at sentences such as the ones below. You should note that in English, various ways are used to express the notion of "by means of". Sometimes the preposition "by" is used on its own; in other cases, the preposition "with" is used. The English could be misleading, and the "with" that we are referring to here should not be confused with the notion of "together with".

I travel to work by bus (literally: by means of the bus)

He is hitting the boy with a stick (literally: by means of a stick)

The prefix that is used in Zulu to express this notion is **"nga"**. As with **"na"**, the vowel **"a"** merges with the following vowel:

nga	+	u	>	ngo
nga	+	i	>	nge
nga	+	a	>	nga

Let's look at a few sentences now:

I go/travel to work by bus (literally: by means of a bus)

Ngiya emsebenzini ngebhasi   (nga + ibhasi)

He is hitting the boy with a stick (literally: by means of a stick)

Ushaya umfana ngenduku   (nga + induku)

This prefix may also be used to convey the notion of "about" in a sentence such as the following:

They are talking about the teacher

Bakhuluma ngothisha   (nga + uthisha)

They are talking about the children

Bakhuluma ngabantwana   (nga + abantwana)

LESSON 7

THE USE OF ADJECTIVES

Adjectives as they are known in English, are qualifying words which tell us more about some or other noun, for example:

> The _tall_ boy
>
> The _big_ house
>
> The _old_ motor car

Adjectives in Zulu are formed by using an adjective (agreement) marker together with a stem. The following is a list of adjective markers. Once again, remember that the marker must agree in class with the noun to which it refers.

CLASS	ADJECTIVE MARKERS
1	om
2	aba
1a	om
2a	aba
3	om
4	emi
5	eli
6	ama
7	esi
8	ezin/ezim
9	en/em
10	ezin/ezim
11	olu
14	obu
15	oku

There are a restricted number of adjective stems in Zulu. At the introductory level, you should concentrate only on the following:

-de	"tall, long"
-fuphi	"short"
-khulu	"big"
-ncane	"small"
-dala	"old"
-sha	"new, young"
-hle	"nice, beautiful"
-ningi	"many, much"

In order to form an adjective, the class of the noun has to be taken into consideration first, so that the correct adjective marker is chosen. This marker is then prefixed to the adjective stem.

Example:

the old teacher

In Zulu, the adjective normally follows the noun,

uthisha   om   +   dala >

uthisha   omdala

The short boy

umfana   om   +   fuphi >

umfana   omfuphi

the old shop

isitolo   esi   +   dala   >

isitolo   esidala

tall people

abantu   aba   +   de   >

abantu   abade

a big school

isikole   esi   +   khulu   >

isikole   esikhulu

the short girl

intombazana   em   +   fuphi   >

intombazana   emfuphi

(In class 9, the marker ending in **m** occurs with **–fuphi**. The same applies to classes 8 and 10.)

Unfortunately, a few additional changes take place with the use of some of these stems, for example:

1.   When the class 1 marker **"om"** is used with the stem **"-de"** or**"-hle"**,

   then:

   "om" changes to **"omu"**, e.g.

   umfana   omu   +   de

   umfana omude   "the tall boy"

   unesi omuhle   "the beautiful nurse"

2.   When the class 9 adjective marker **"en-"** is used with the stem **"sha"**, then,

"**-sha**" becomes **"tsha"**. (the same applies to classes 8 and 10.)

indlu   en   +   sha   >   indlu entsha

"the new house"

3.   When the class 9 adjective maker **"en-"** is used with the stem **"-khulu"**, then **"khulu"** becomes **"-kulu"**. The actual effect here is a reduction in the "forcefulness" of the sound **"kh"**. (The same applies with the markers of classes 8 and 10.)

indlu   en   +   khulu >   indlu enkulu

"the big house"

izindlu   ezin +   khulu >   izindlu ezinkulu

"the big houses"

Adjectives used predicatively

When you want to use an adjective in a predicative sense, in other words if you want to say:

The person is old

...then, you simply omit the initial vowel of the adjectival marker, thus:

umuntu omdala   >   **umuntu mdala**

the old person   the person is old

isikole esikhulu   >   **isikole sikhulu**

the big school   the school is big

abantu abaningi   >   **abantu baningi**

many people   the people are many

In class 9 however, the subject agreement marker replaces the initial vowel of the adjectival marker:

indlu enhle   >   indlu   i + nhle >   **indlu inhle**

the nice house   the house is nice

imoto enkulu   >   imoto   i + nkulu >   **imoto inkulu**

the big motor car   the motor car is big

The use of qualifying words in Zulu is not as straightforward as in English. When certain qualifying words are used, the markers are slightly different in some of the classes. This is the case with qualifying words such as the following:*

(*Traditionally, these have been called "relatives")

-mnyama   "black"

-mhlophe   "white"

-nsundu   "brown"

-bomvu   "red"

-bukhali   "sharp"

-buthuntu   "blunt:

-banzi   "wide"

When the above are used, then the markers of the following classes are different from the list given earlier. These are, in general, shortened forms.

Class:

1	omu	>	o
3	omu	>	o
4	emi	>	e
6	ama	>	a
9	en/em	>	e
10	ezin/ezim	>	ezi

The markers of the other classes remain the same.

(2 aba,   5 eli,   7 esi,   8 ezi   11 olu,   14 obu, 15 oku)

Imoto emnyama

The black motor car

Ihembe elimhlophe

The white shirt

Umese obukhali

The sharp knife

Another way of expressing the English adjective

In Zulu, there is yet another way of expressing the English adjective. In some cases, the marker is added to a verb stem, to be more specific, a verb which expresses a state.

So, for example, if one wanted to translate the English "the sick boy", then in Zulu one would have to first rephrase this as "the boy who is sick".

In such instances the markers of the last list above are added to the verb stem. A suffix **"yo"** is then added.

o + gula + yo

Hence the full form is:

Umfana ogulayo

Look at the following examples as well:

The sick boys   **abafana abagulayo**

                  < aba + gula + yo

The hot tea   **itiye elishisayo**

                  < eli + shisa + yo

It does happen sometimes that the English adjective which is used, translates a Zulu verb which takes the **"-ile"** suffix, or its variant forms. This is because we are dealing here with states and as was noted earlier, certain verbs in Zulu take on these suffixes when they express a present state.

Thus:

the hungry boy

is translated as:

the boy who is hungry

umfana o + lambile + yo
➢ **umfana olambileyo**

the thirsty students

izitshudeni ez + omile + yo
➢ **ezomileyo**

the tired teacher

uthisha o + khathele + yo
➢ **okhatheleyo**

LESSON 8

SENTENCES IN THE NEGATIVE

Up until now, we have looked at sentences which have been in the positive form. In this lesson, we will look at ways in which negative statements can be made. The three tenses which we will concentrate on, are the Present, Future and Past.

The Present Tense

In this lesson, we are interested in expressing statements such as:

the boy is not drinking water

the teachers are not running

the girl is not leaving

The pattern in the negative is as follows:

a - AM - Verb Stem

The initial **"a"** in this pattern is commonly referred to as the negative prefix. This is followed by an agreement marker (**AM**); then comes the verb stem with the suffix **"i"**.

Unfortunately, the agreement markers in the negative tenses differ in some classes from the positive ones.

Negative Agreement Markers

Class	
1	ka
2	ba
1a	ka
2a	ba
3	wu
4	yi
5	li
6	wa
7	si
8	zi
9	yi
10	zi
11	lu
14	bu
15	ku

First person	sg	**ngi**
First person	pl	**si**
Second person	sg	**wu**
Second person	pl	**ni**
Third person	sg	**ka**
Third person	pl	**ba**

(Generally speaking, the forms of the Third person singular and plural are the same as those of classes 1 and 2 respectively. However, if the subject noun belongs to another class, then the agreement marker of that class will be used.)

Note that these agreement markers are used for all three tenses, namely the present, future and past.

The reason why some of the above markers differ from the positive ones is because of the initial negative prefix **"a"**. As you know, two vowels may not occur next to one another in Zulu, and for this reason a semi-vowel such as **"w"** or **"y"** is usually added to the agreement marker.

Thus for example the positive agreement marker of class 3 changes as follows:

Class 3:   Positive   =   **u**

                Negative   =   **a** (neg. pr.) **+ u**   **> a + wu**

Note that class 1 (or 3rd person singular) is an exception here; the positive form **"u"** changes to **"ka"** and not to the expected **"wu"**.

Let's take our earlier examples and attempt to translate them. (There is no distinction between a long and a short form in the negative.)

The boy is not drinking water

umfana   **a + ka + phuz + i   amanzi**   **>**

umfana akaphuzi amanzi

The teachers are not running

othisha   **a + ba + gijim + i >**

othisha abagijimi

The girl is not leaving

Intombazana   a + yi + hamb + i   >

Intombazana ayihambi

Note the corresponding negative forms below:

umfana ufunda isiZulu   "the boy studies Zulu"
> **umfana akafundi isiZulu**

abafana bafunda isiZulu   "the boys study Zulu"
> **abafana abafundi isiZulu**

iphoyisa lifunda isiZulu   "the policeman studies Zulu"
> **iphoyisa alifundi isiZulu**

amaphoyisa afunda isiZulu   "the policemen study Zulu"
> **amaphoyisa awafundi isiZulu**

isisebenzi sifunda isiZulu   "the servant studies Zulu"
> **isisebenzi asifundi isiZulu**

izisebenzi zifunda isiZulu   "the servants study Zulu"
> **izisebenzi azifundi isiZulu**

insizwa ifunda isiZulu   "the young man studies Zulu"
> **insizwa ayifundi isiZulu**

izinsizwa zifunda isiZulu   "the young men study Zulu"
> **izinsizwa azifundi isiZulu**

Now translate each of the following sentences into Zulu:

1. Sipho is not studying

2. The doctor is not leaving

3. My brother is not ill

4. The girl is not cooking

5. My mother is not studying Zulu

6. Thandi is not buying milk

7. The lazy person is not sick

8. The boys are not crying

9. I am not cooking meat

10. You are not working

Answers:

1. **USipho akafundi**

2. **Udokotela akahambi**

3. **Umfowethu akaguli**

4. **Intombazana ayipheki**

5. **Umama akafundi isiZulu**

6. **UThandi akathengi ubisi**

7. **Ivila aliguli**

8. **Abafana abakhali**

9. **Angipheki inyama**

10. **Awusebenzi**

The Future Negative

The future negative is formed in the following way:

a - AM - zu - Verb Stem

Note here that the negative agreement marker is followed by **"zu"** (as opposed to the positive **"zo"**. The verb stem here ends in **"a"**).

So for example:

Abafana bazofunda isiZulu

The boys will study Zulu

becomes

Abafana abazufunda isiZulu

The boys will not study Zulu

Let's look at a few more examples:

1.   Sipho will not study

2.   The doctor will not leave

3.   My brother will not eat

4.   The girl will not cook

5.   My mother will not study Zulu

6.   Thandi will not buy milk

7.   The lazy person will not run

8.   The boys will not cry

9.   I will not cook meat

10.   You will not work

Answers:

1.   **USipho akazufunda**

2.   **Udokotela akazuhamba**

3.   **Umfowethu akazukudla**

        (Note that when the stem is monosyllabic, then **"ku"** is usually inserted before the stem, thus **"ku"** + **"dla"**)

4.   **Intombazana ayizupheka**

5.   **Umama akazufunda isiZulu**

6.   **UThandi akazuthenga ubisi**

7.   **Ivila alizugijima**

8.   **Abafana abazukhala**

9.   **Angizupheka inyama**

10.   **Awuzusebenza**

The Past Tense

The negative of the past tense is formed in the following way:

a - AM - Verb Stem

Here the final suffix **"a"** of the verb stem is replaced by **"anga"**

Thus:

a - ngi - fund - anga > angifundanga

Translates: I have not studied   OR

                     I did not study

Now translate the following sentences:

1.   Sipho did not study

2.   The doctor has not left

3.   My brother has not eaten

4.   The girl did not cook

5.   My mother did not study Zulu

6.   Thandi has not bought milk

7.   The lazy person did not run

8.   The boys did not cry

9.   I did not cook meat

10.   You have not worked

Answers

1.   **USipho akafundanga**

2.   **Udokotela akahambanga**

3.   **Umfowethu akadlanga**

4.   **Intombazana ayiphekanga**

5.   **Umama akafundanga isiZulu**

6.   **UThandi akathenganga ubisi**

7.   **Ivila aligijimanga**

8.   **Abafana abakhalanga**

9.   **Angiphekanga inyama**

10.   **Awusebenzanga**

You may remember that in the positive of the past tense, there are a few roots which take on certain special suffixes, in order to express states. In the negative form, these suffixes remain the same.

ngikhathele	>	**angikhathele**
I am tired		I am not tired
uthukuthele	>	**awuthukuthele**
you are angry		you are not angry
balambile	>	**abalambile**
they are hungry		they are not hungry
ulele	>	**akalele**
she is sleeping		she is not sleeping

LESSON 9

THE USE OF PRONOUNS

We have noted in earlier lessons, that an agreement marker can be used in sentences to translate what we would normally call 'pronouns' in English. Thus for example, the pronoun **"I"** would be translated by the agreement marker **"ngi"** in the following sentence:

Ngifuna ukudla

I want to eat

These markers are not independent words in Zulu. They are prefixes which occur within words.

It is also possible to use independent pronouns in Zulu. These are independent words, unlike the markers above. Let's look at the list below. As is to be expected, there is a pronoun for every person and class as well.

First person singular	**mina**
First person plural	**thina**
Second person singular	**wena**
Second person plural	**nina**
Third person singular	**yena**
Third person plural	**bona**

Class:		
	1	**yena**
	2	**bona**
	1a	**yena**

2a	bona
3	wona
4	yona
5	lona
6	wona
7	sona
8	zona
9	yona
10	zona
11	lona
14	bona
15	khona

These pronouns are usually used when one wishes to emphasise the person or object concerned, or when one wishes to introduce an element of contrast. Thus for example, one would say:

Mina, ngizohamba   "As for me, I will leave"

Note here that even though we use a pronoun **"mina"** to translate 'I", the agreement marker **"ngi"** is obligatorily used in the verb as well. In a sense, we have two items, so to speak, which translate "I" - the personal pronoun, **"mina"** and the agreement marker **"ngi".**

The pronoun may be used together with the noun for emphasis purposes. Sometimes it is difficult to translate an emphatic form, since, as we know, the mere raising of the voice can have the same effect. In the sentences below this is illustrated by underlining the English pronoun.

Umfana yena uzosala; wena uzohamba

As for the boy, <u>he</u> will stay behind. <u>You</u> will leave.

Ufuna ubani?   **"Ufuna wena"**

Whom does he want?   "He wants <u>you</u>"

Yena, akasebenzi kahle   "As for him, <u>he</u> does not work well"

Bona, abasebenzi kahle   "As for them, <u>they</u> do not work well"

Note the following combinations:

umfana	**yena**
abafana	**bona**
ubaba	**yena**
obaba	**bona**
umfula	**wona**
imifula	**yona**
ivila	**lona**
amavila	**wona**
isisebenzi	**sona**
izisebenzi	**zona**
imoto	**yona**
izimoto	**zona**
ubisi	**lona**
ubusuku	**bona**
ukudla	**khona**

LESSON 10

EXPRESSING "THIS", "THAT", "THOSE", ETC

In a discourse situation, the need sometimes arises for the speaker to point out persons or objects. This is achieved by using what are commonly referred to as deictic expressions or demonstratives.

As is to be expected, there is a demonstrative for each class in Zulu, and one always needs to know the noun that is being referred to.

In English, the types of expressions that are used are, for example, "this", "these", "that", "those", etc.

In Zulu, we conveniently recognize three different positions for such expressions, namely:

Position 1   -   translating "this", "these"

Position 2   -   translating "that", "those"

Position 3   -   translating "that/those over there in the distance"

CLASS	POSITION 1	POSITION 2	POSITION 3
1	lo	lowo	lowaya
2	laba	labo	labaya
1a	lo	lowo	lowaya
2a	laba	labo	labaya
3	lo	lowo	lowaya
4	le	leyo	leya
5	leli	lelo	leliya
6	la	lawo	lawaya
7	lesi	leso	lesiya
8	lezi	lezo	leziya
9	le	leyo	leya
10	lezi	lezo	leziya
11	lolu	lolo	loluya
14	lobu	lobo	lobuya
15	lokhu	lokho	lokhuya

The demonstrative in Zulu usually occurs before the noun, although it can also be used after it.

When the demonstrative occurs before the noun, the initial vowel of the noun is deleted.

Lo mfana uyagula   "This boy is ill"

Ngifuna leso sitsha   "I want that dish"

Laba bafana   "These boys"

Laba bantwana	"These children"
Leli tafula	"This table"
Le moto	"This motor-car"
Lezi moto	"These motor-cars"
Leli kati	"This cat"
Amabhuku lawo	"Those books"
Abantwana labaya	"Those children over there"
Isitshudeni lesi	"This student"
Izitshudeni lezo	"Those students"

LESSON 11

EXPRESSING THE GENITIVE

The genitive is a construction which generally expresses some or other form of possession, for example:

the boy's dog

In Zulu, the above ordering is changed around. This order is also possible in English

the dog of the boy

In this example, that which is owned comes first (i.e. the dog) followed by the person who owns it (i.e. the boy).

We have no prepositions in Zulu, and as is to be expected a genitive *marker* is used to express the concept "of". This marker is attached to the second noun.

Here follows a list of genitive, or 'possessive' markers as they are sometimes called.

CLASS	
1	wa
2	ba
1a	wa
2a	ba
3	wa
4	ya
5	la
6	a
7	sa
8	za
9	ya
10	za
11	lwa
14	ba
15	kwa

When the marker occurs before the noun then a merging of vowels takes place, whereby the vowel **"a"** of the marker merges with the first vowel of the following noun:

Let's take our example once again.

The word for dog is **"inja"** which belongs to class 9, thus the genitive marker which agrees with it is **"ya"**. This **"ya"** is then attached to the noun **"umfana"**; a merging of the vowels then takes place:

inja   ya   +   umfana   >

inja yomfana

The three basic rules of merging as we have already seen are:

a   +   u   >   o

a   +   i   >   e

a   +   a   >   a

Now let's look at the following examples:

The cat of the lazy person

ikati la + ivila >

ikati levila

the cat of the girls

ikati la + amantombazana >

ikati lamantombazana

the money of the people

imali ya + abantu >

imali yabantu

the money of the servant

imali ya + isisebenzi >

imali yesisebenzi

Where the second noun is a noun of class 2a, then the vowel of the genitive marker is merely deleted.

The dog of the teachers

inja ya + othisha >

inja yothisha

The money of the nurses

imali ya + onesi >

imali yonesi

Unfortunately, as is so often the case, exceptions occur, and this can also be seen in the genitive when the noun in second position is a noun of class 1a. Nouns in this class are those such as: **ubaba, umama, unesi, uthisha, etc.**

When the noun in first position contains a prefix with a nasal in it, i.e. **"m"** or **"n"**, then **"ka"** is used as a genitive marker, and the vowel of the noun is deleted.

the child of the nurse

umntwana ka + unesi > umntwana kanesi

the money of the nurse

imali ka + unesi > imali kanesi

the dog of my father

inja ka + ubaba > inja kababa

When the *initial* noun belongs to the other classes, then the genitive marker is made up of the agreement marker + **"ka"**:

the children of Thandi

abantwana ba + ka + uThandi >

abantwana bakaThandi

the chairs of the teacher

izitulo zi + ka + uthisha >

izitulo zikathisha

Expressing "my, "your", "his", etc.

Here we use the personal pronouns which we saw earlier. However, these pronouns change in this construction as follows:

First person singular	**mina**	**>**	**-mi**
First person plural	**thina**	**>**	**-ethu**
Second person singular	**wena**	**>**	**-kho**
Second person plural	**nina**	**>**	**-enu**
Third person singular/Class 1	**yena**	**>**	**-khe**

Examples:

izimoto zethu (< za + ethu)	our motor cars
abantwana benu (< ba + enu)	your children
imali yakhe	his money
imoto yami	my motor-car
umsebenzi wakho	your work
isitulo sakhe	his chair
igama lakho	your name

As for the rest of the classes, the pronoun is used (without the **"-na"**).

izimoto zabo	their motor cars (referring to **"abantwana"**)
imali yaso	her money (referring to **"isisebenzi"**)
ibhuku lalo	his book (referring to **"ivila"**)
amabhuku azo	their books (referring to **"izitshudeni"**)
isinkwa sabo	their bread (referring to **"abafana"**)
inyama yaso	his meat (referring to **"isitshudeni"**)
izinja zabo	their dogs (referring to **"othisha"**)

LESSON 12

NOTES ON OTHER CONSTRUCTIONS

(a) Identifying oneself

In order to translate expressions such as:

I am a teacher

....the verb agreement marker (AM) is used, followed by an 'identifying' prefix (IP) and then the noun. The identifying prefix varies, but the general rule is that if the following noun begins with the vowels **"u"**, **"o"**, **"a"**, then the prefix used is **"ng"**; if the noun begins with the vowel **"i"**, then the prefix used is **"y"**.

I am a teacher

ngi (AM) + ng (IP) + uthisha > nginguthisha

he is a doctor

u + ng + udokotela > ungudokotela

they are doctors

ba + ng + odokotela > bangodokotela

he is a lazy person

u + y + ivila > uyivila

he is a thief

u + y + isela > uyisela

they are thieves

ba + ng + amasela > bangamasela

she is a servant

u + y + isisebenzi > uyisisebenzi

If one uses the indefinite "it" in subject position, then in Zulu the agreement marker is left out:

it is my money

y + imali yami > yimali yami

it is water

ng + amanzi > ngamanzi

it's my brother

ng + umfowethu > ngumfowethu

(b)   Expressing "and"

When one wishes to express the conjunction "and" between two nouns such as in:

Thandi and Themba

....then the prefix **"na"** is used before the second noun. Once again the rules of merging take place, whereby:

na + u > no

na + i > ne

na + a > na

uThandi na + uThemba > uThandi noThemba

the nurse and the man

unesi na + indoda > unesi nendoda

the boys and the girls

abafana na + amantombazana > abafana namantombazana

When the conjunction "and" is used to combine two clauses in English, the conjunction **"futhi"** is used in Zulu:

Umama upheka ukudla futhi abantwana badlala phandle

(**dlala** play; **phandle** outside)

My mother is cooking food and the children are playing outside

(c) Expressing the concept "here it is"

A single word is used to express this concept, but as in many other cases, the word has to agree in class with the noun referred to. The more common classes are given here.

Iphi imali yami?	Where is my money?
Nansi	Here it is
Uphi uThandi?	Where is Thandi?
Nangu	Here she is
Baphi abantwana?	Where are the children?
Nampa	Here they are

Consider the forms for the classes below:

Class:

1.	nangu	umfana
2.	nampa/naba	abafana
1a.	nangu	ubaba
2a.	nampa/naba	obaba
3.	nanku	umfula
4.	nansi/nayi	imifula
5.	nanti/nali	ivila
6.	nanka	amavila
7.	nasi	isitshudeni

8.	nazi	izitshudeni
9.	nansi/nayi	imoto
10.	nazi	izimoto
11.	nantu/nalu	ufudu
14.	nampu	utshani
15.	nakhu	ukudla

(d)   Expressing "should"

Here the **AM** is followed by the verb stem which ends in **"e"** and not **"a"**.

Ngihambe na?   <   ngi + hambe

Should I go?

Sivale amafasitela na? <   si + vale

Should we close the windows?

Ngibuye kusasa na?   <   ngi +buye

Should I return tomorrow?

(e)   Expressing an object in the verb

We have seen basic sentences where the object occurs after the verb as in:

Umfana ufunda isiZulu

The boy is studying Zulu

In a discourse situation, one might not need to refer to the object noun, in which case a pronoun may be used, e.g.

The boy is studying it

We have seen pronouns in Zulu, and in this case the form which would agree with **"isiZulu"** would be **"sona"**. However, the use of the pronoun in Zulu creates emphasis. If a mere statement were to be made such as in the example above, then one can use what is called an *object* agreement marker before the verb stem. (The long form of the present tense is then used.)

Umfana u + ya + si + funda

Umfana uyasifunda

Here the **"si"** form is the so-called object agreement marker. Remember the long form is used because there is no *object noun* occurring *after* the verb in Zulu. The object is represented by an agreement marker in the verb.

Here is a complete list of object agreement markers for each of the persons and classes.

First person singular	**ngi**
First person plural	**si**
Second person singular	**ku**
Second person plural	**ni**
Third person singular	**m**
Third person plural	**ba**

Class:	
1	m
2	ba
1a	m
2a	ba
3	wu
4	yi
5	li
6	wa
7	si
8	zi
9	yi
10	zi
11	lu
14	bu
15	ku

Now try the following:

(i)   I will see you (singular) tomorrow

(ii)   I will see them tomorrow   (with reference to **"abantwana"**)

(iii)   They like me

(iv)   She likes you (singular)

(v)   The teacher wants to see her   (with reference to **"ivila"**)

(vi)   I bought it yesterday   (with reference to **"isinkwa"**)

(vii)   We bought it yesterday   (with reference to **"imoto"**)

Answers

(i)   **Ngizo<u>ku</u>bona kusasa**

(ii)   **Ngizo<u>ba</u>bona kusasa**

(iii)   **Baya<u>ngi</u>thanda**

(iv)   **Uya<u>ku</u>thanda**

(v)   **Uthisha ufuna uku<u>li</u>bona**

(vi)   **Ngi<u>si</u>thengile izolo**

(vii)   **Si<u>yi</u>thengile izolo**

(f)   Asking the question "why?"

In an earlier lesson, we dealt with certain questions, but it was felt that it would be best to leave this particular kind of question till now, since it involves a special type of verb construction.

When asking the question "why?", the introductory word **"yini?"** is first used followed by a verb with the following structure:

In the positive:

Yini + AM - Verb stem

(however, in classes 1, 2 and 6 the subject agreement markers are **e, be** and **e** respectively.)

Yini ukhala?	Why are you crying?
Yini ekhala?	Why is he crying?
Yini bekhala?	Why are they crying?

Yini abantwana bekhala?   Why are the children crying?

Yini ivila likhala?   Why is the lazy person crying?

(Note that there is no **"ya"** long form in the verb when this question is asked.)

In the negative:

The construction is as follows:

Yini + AM - nga - verb stem (ending in **"i"**)

Yini ungasebenzi?   Why are you not working?

Yini engasebenzi?   Why is he not working?

Yini bengasebenzi?   Why are they not working?

Yini abafana bengasebenzi?   Why are the boys not working?

Yini ivila lingasebenzi?   Why is the lazy person not working?

(g)   Expressing the concept "have/have not"

Here we are looking at expressions such as:

I have money

I have a motor car

Do you have money?

In this construction we use the relevant (subject) agreement marker followed by the prefix **"na"** and then the noun, thus:

AM + na + noun

Ngi + na + imali

The vowel of **"na"** then merges with the initial vowel of the following noun, thus:

nginemali   I have money

Remember the three rules of vowel merging:

na + a > na

na + i > ne

na + u > no

I have a motor car

Nginemoto

Do you have money?

Unemali na?

She has children

Unabantwana

We have dogs

Sinezinja

I have tobacco

Nginogwayi

In the negative, the vowel of **"na"** is retained and the vowel of the noun is deleted. The negative prefix **"a"** occurs at the beginning of the construction.

a + AM + na + noun (with deletion of the initial vowel)

a + ngi + na + imali   **> anginamali**

                    I don't have money

a + ngi + na + imoto   **> anginamoto**

                    I don't have a motor car

a + ka + na + abantwana > akanabantwana

                    She doesn't have children

(h)   Expressing the idea of "to be at a place"

Here we are looking at expressions such as:

He is in Johannesburg

He is at home

I am at work

Although there are a number of rules governing this type of construction, the most common formation is to use the subject agreement marker, followed by the consonant **"s"** and then the adverb of place.

u + s + eGoli >

useGoli

u + s + ekhaya >

usekhaya

ngi + s + emsebenzini >

ngisemsebenzini

The negative is formed as follows. Remember to use the negative agreement marker:

a + AM + s + Adverb of place

akaseGoli

akasekhaya

angisemsebenzini

(i)   Expressing the idea of "doing something for, on behalf of"

As we have already seen, there are no prepositions in Zulu, which means of course that there are no separate words for prepositions. Instead prefixes and suffixes are used to express the English preposition.

When one wishes to express the idea of "for" then a change takes place in the verb stem, for example:

We know that the stem **"sebenza"** means "work". Now if we replace the final **"a"** with **"ela"**, then the idea of "for" is expressed.

Basebenza eGoli   They work in Johannesburg

but

Basebenzela ubaba   They work for my father

Ngithenga isinkwa   I am buying bread

but

Ngithengela umama isinkwa

Literally: I am buying – for mother- bread

I am buying bread for my mother

SOME COMMON EXPRESSIONS

Here are some common expressions that you might like to learn by heart. Many of them involve constructions which have been dealt with in the course of our lessons. (You might like to analyse the constructions while going through these expressions.)

Thank you

Ngiyabonga	Thank you
Ngibonga kakhulu	Thank you very much

What do you want?

Ufunani?	What do you want? (singular)
Nifunani?	What do you want? (plural)

Come here!

Woza lapha!	Come here! (singular)
Wozani lapha!	Come here! (plural)

Where are you going?

Uyaphi?	Where are you going? (singular)
Niyaphi?	Where are you going? (plural)

Time

Isikhathi sithini?   What is the time?

Literally: "time says what"

or

Yisikhathi sini?

Ngu- 4   It is 4 o'clock

Nguphasi 4   It is half past 4

Enquiring about one's name

Igama lakho ngubani?   What is your name?

Literally: "name – yours is whom?"

or

Ngubani igama lakho?

or

Ungubani (igama lakho)?

Igama lami nguJohn   My name is John

Literally: "name – mine is John"

or

NginguJohn

Isibongo sakho ngubani?   What is your surname?

or

Ngubani isibongo sakho?

Isibongo sami nguJones   My surname is Jones

Sorry

Uxolo   Sorry, pardon me, excuse me

or

Ngiyaxolisa

Weather

(Note that when translating the English indefinite form "it" in a verb, the Zulu marker **ku** is used).

Kuyashisa namhlanje	It is hot today
Kuyabanda namhlanje	It is cold today

Intention / Wanting

Ngifuna ukuthenga isinkwa	I want to buy bread
Ngifuna ukuthenga ubisi	I want to buy milk
Ngifuna amanzi	I want water
Ingane ifuna amanzi	The child (infant) wants water

Requests

Mawungene!	Please enter! (singular)
Maningene!	Please enter! (plural)
Mawuvule amafasitela!	Please open the windows! (singular)
Manivule amafasitela!	Please open the windows! (plural)
Mawuvale amafasitela!	Please close the windows! (singular)
Manivale amafasitela!	Please close the windows! (plural)

Mawungabhemi!	Please do not smoke! (singular)
Maningabhemi!	Please do not smoke! (plural)

Makalinde!	Let her wait!
Makasebenze!	Let her work!

Cost

Yimalini?	How much (does it cost)?
Yimalini otamatisi?	How much are the tomatoes?

Yi – R2   (It costs) two Rand

Literally: It is R2

or

Ngamarandi amabili   (It costs) two Rand

Literally: It is Rands-two

Be able to / can

(Uyakwazi + uku-verb stem + na?)

Uyakwazi ukupheka na?   Can you cook?

Literally: Are you able to cook?

Uyakwazi ukubhukuda na?   Can you swim?

Uyakwazi ukushayela imoto?   Can you drive?

See you again!

Ngizokubona futhi	I'll see you again
Ngizokubona kusasa	I'll see you tomorrow

Days of the week

Ngizokubona	**+**	**ngoMsombuluko**	on Monday
I shall see you		**ngoLwesibili**	on Tuesday
		ngoLwesithathu	on Wednesday
		ngoLwesine	on Thursday
		ngoLwesihlanu	on Friday
		ngoMgqibelo	on Saturday
		ngeSonto	on Sunday

Where is ... ?

Umama wakho uphi?	Where is your mother?
Uthisha uphi?	Where is the teacher?
Abantwana baphi?	Where are the children?
Umama usemsebenzini	Mother is at work
Uthisha usesikoleni	The teacher is at school
Abantwana basekhaya	The children are at home

How do you travel (by what means)?

Uya emsebenzini ngani?	How do you go to work?

Literally: "You go to work by means of what?"

Ngiya emsebenzini ngebhasi	I go to work by bus
Ngiya emsebenzini ngemoto	I go to work by car
Ngiya emsebenzini ngesitimela	I go to work by train

Do you know him?

(the object agreement marker + **-azi** know)

Uyamazi uJoji?	Do you know George?
Yebo, ngiyamazi	Yes, I know him
Cha, angimazi	No, I don't know him

(More on) Time

Uzofika nini?	When will you arrive?
Ngizofika ngo- 9	I shall arrive at 9
Bazobuya ngo- 10	They will return at 10

Who? (in subject position)

Ngubani osebenza lapha? (**o** = adjective marker before verb stems)

Literally: It is who, who is working here?

Who is working here?

Ngubani ohlala lapha?

Literally: It is who, who lives here?   >   Who lives here?

What language do you speak?

Ukhulumani?	What language do you speak?
Ngikhuluma isiNgisi	I speak English
Ngikhuluma isiZulu	I speak Zulu
Ngikhuluma isiBhunu	I speak Afrikaans
Ngikhuluma isiXhosa	I speak Xhosa

Asking for something

 (verb stem: -cela + object)

Ngicela ukudla	I am asking for food
Ngicela imali	I am asking for money

Granting Permission (may)

(AM - nga - verb stem)

Ungangena	You (singular) may come in
Ungadlala phandle	You (singular) may play outside
Ningahlala phasi	You (plural) may sit down

Miscellaneous other expressions

Ngiyakuthanda	I like you
Ushadile na?	Are you married?
Mehlomadala /	
Angisakwazi	Long time no see
Unamanga/ukhuluma amanga	You are telling lies
Yiqiniso	It is the truth
UJabulani ukhona na?	Is Jabulani present?
Udokotela ukhona na?	Is the doctor present?
Unesi ukhona na?	Is the nurse present?
Yebo ukhona	Yes he/she is (present)
Cha, akekho	No, he/she isn't

Some common exclamations

Hhayi! / hhayibo! / hhayi khona!	No! (definite denial)
We!	Hey!
We bantwana! Thulani!	Hey children! Keep quiet!
Hawu!	Expression of wonder
	(my word, hurrah, good heavens)
Hawu! Bafikile	My word! They have arrived
Awu!	My!
Awu! Uphasile Thandi	My! You have passed, Thandi!

(When speaking directly to a person, the initial class prefix **u** is elided, thus
uThandi becomes **Thandi**)

Bibliography

Crystal. D. 1992 *An Encyclopedic Dictionary of Language and Languages.* Oxford: Blackwell.

Doke C.M. 1945 *Textbook of Zulu Grammar.* London: Longmans, Green & Co.

Hendrikse, A.P. & G. Poulos 1994. "Word Categories – Prototypes and Continua in Southern Bantu." *Southern African Journal of Linguistics,* Supplement 20: 215-245.

Poulos G. 1982 *"Issues in Zulu Relativization" Communication No. 11* (Published Ph.D Thesis). Grahamstown: Rhodes University.

Poulos, G. 1990 *A Linguistic Analysis of Venda.* Pretoria: Via Afrika.

Poulos, G. & L.J. Louwrens 1994 *A Linguistic Analysis of Northern Sotho.* Pretoria: Via Afrika

Poulos, G. & C.T. Msimang 1998 *A Linguistic Analysis of Zulu.* Cape Town: Via Afrika

Wilkes, A & N. Nkosi 1995 *Zulu: A complete course for beginners.* London: Hodder Headline

Made in the USA
Monee, IL
03 December 2023

48049351R10063